Best Practices for Teaching
SCIENCE

Other Books by Randi Stone

Best Practices for Teaching Mathematics: What Award-Winning Classroom Teachers Do, 2007

Best Practices for Teaching Writing: What Award-Winning Classroom Teachers Do, 2007

Best Classroom Management Practices for Reaching All Learners: What Award-Winning Classroom Teachers Do, 2005

Best Teaching Practices for Reaching All Learners: What Award-Winning Classroom Teachers Do, 2004

What?! Another New Mandate? What Award-Winning Teachers Do When School Rules Change, 2002

Best Practices for High School Classrooms: What Award-Winning Secondary Teachers Do, 2001

Best Classroom Practices: What Award-Winning Elementary Teachers Do, 1999

New Ways to Teach Using Cable Television: A Step-by-Step Guide, 1997

Best Practices for Teaching

SCIENCE

What Award-Winning Classroom Teachers Do

RANDI STONE

Skyhorse Publishing

Copyright © 2007 by Corwin Press
First Skyhorse Publishing edition 2015

Skyhorse Publishing books may be purchased in bulk at special discounts for sales promotion, corporate gifts, fund-raising, or educational purposes. Special editions can also be created to specifications. For details, contact the Special Sales Department, Skyhorse Publishing, 307 West 36th Street, 11th Floor, New York, NY 10018 or info@skyhorsepublishing.com.

Skyhorse® and Skyhorse Publishing® are registered trademarks of Skyhorse Publishing, Inc.®, a Delaware corporation.

Visit our website at www.skyhorsepublishing.com.

10 9 8 7 6 5 4 3 2 1

Library of Congress Cataloging-in-Publication Data is available on file.

Cover design by Scott Van Atta

Print ISBN: 978-1-63220-545-2
Ebook ISBN: 978-1-63220-962-7

Printed in the United States of America

Contents

Preface

In the pages that follow, award-winning teachers generously share their best teaching practices with us. I hope you enjoy reading about their classrooms and trying out their teaching techniques as much as I have.

⧉ Acknowledgments

Thank you to a wonderful group of teachers for sharing your stories with us.

About the Author

 **Randi Stone** is a graduate of Clark University, Boston University, and Salem State College. She completed her doctorate in education at the University of Massachusetts, Lowell. She is the author of nine books with Corwin Press, including her latest in a series: *Best Practices for Teaching Writing: What Award-Winning Classroom Teachers Do, Best Practices for Teaching Mathematics: What Award-Winning Classroom Teachers Do,* and *Best Practices for Teaching Science: What Award-Winning Classroom Teachers Do.* She lives with her teenage daughter, Blair, in Keene, New Hampshire.

About the
Contributors

Frieda Taylor Aiken, Gifted Teacher
Jackson Elementary School
218 Woodland Way
Jackson, Georgia 30233
School Telephone Number: (770) 504-2320
E-mail: aikenf@butts.k12.ga.us

Number of Years Teaching: 18
Awards: Toyota Tapestry Mini-Grant, Environmental Science
Education, "Ecology in a Box," 2005
Teacher of the Year, Jackson Elementary School,
2000–2001
District Georgia Science Teacher of the Year,
2000–2001

Douglas L. Bailer, PhD, Mathematics/Science Teacher
Earnest Pruett Center of Technology
29490 U.S. Highway 72
Hollywood, Alabama 35752
School Telephone Number: (256) 574-6079
E-mail: bailerd@jackson.k12.al.us

Number of Years Teaching: 16
Award: Alpha Award for Teaching Excellence, 2000

Cindy Corlett, Building Resource Teacher
Sierra Middle School
6651 Pine Lane Avenue
Parker, Colorado 80138
School Telephone Number: (303) 387-3851
E-mail: cindy.corlett@dcsdk12.org

Number of Years Teaching: 16
Awards: Disney Teacher Honoree, 2005
          Milken National Educator, 2003

Nancy Elliott, Science Teacher
Chillicothe Middle School
1529 Calhoun Street
Chillicothe, Missouri 64601
School Telephone Number: (660) 646-1916
E-mail: nelliott@chillicotheschools.org

Number of Years Teaching: 20
Awards: Regional and State Conservation Teacher of the Year,
          2006
          Disney Teacher Award, 2005
          Water Educator of the Year, 2005
          Vernier Technology Award, 2005
          Toyota TIME Grant recipient, 2005
          Toyota Tapestry Grant recipient, 2006

Mark Goldner, Science Teacher
Heath School
100 Eliot Street
Brookline, Massachusetts 02467
School Telephone Number: (617) 879-4570
E-mail: mark_goldner@brookline.k12.ma.us

Number of Years Teaching: 13
Award: NSTA/Toyota Tapestry Grant for Teachers, 1999

Jason E. Hughes, Agriscience Teacher
St. Marys High School
Route 1 Box 106C
Ravenswood, West Virginia 26164
School Telephone Number: (304) 684-2421
E-mail: jehughes@access.k12.wv.us

Number of Years Teaching: 13
Awards: National Association of Agricultural Educators
Outstanding Teacher, 2005
West Virginia Teacher of the Year, 2005
Distinguished Young Alumnus, West Virginia
University College of Agriculture, Forestry
and Consumer Sciences, 2005

Peter M. Menth, Teacher, Expeditionary Learning Science and Mathematics
Mountain Shadows Middle School
7165 Burton Avenue
Rohnert Park, California 94928
School Telephone Number: (707) 792-4800
E-mail: pmenth@sonic.net

Number of Years Teaching: 9
Award: Toyota Tapestry Grant

Sally Ogilvie, First-Grade Teacher
Syracuse Elementary
1503 South 2000 West
Syracuse, Utah 84075
School Telephone Number: (801) 402-2600
E-mail: sogilvie@dsdmail.net

Number of Years Teaching: 20
Awards: Toyota Tapestry Award, 2005
Agriculture in the Classroom Utah Teacher of
the Year, 2003
National Presidential Award for Excellence in
Elementary Science, 1999

Deborah Perryman, Science Teacher
Elgin High School
1200 Maroon Drive
Elgin, Illinois 60120
School Telephone Number: (847) 888-5100
E-mail: debbieperryman@u-46.org

Number of Years Teaching: 14
Awards: Ten Outstanding Young People of Illinois, 2006
Illinois Teacher of the Year, 2005
National River Hero, River Network, 2005

Lindsey Prentice, Fifth-Grade Teacher
Evansville Lutheran School
120 East Michigan Street
Evansville, Indiana 47711
School Telephone Number: (812) 424-7252

Number of Years Teaching: 6
Awards: Best Buy Teacher Award, 2005
Toyota Tapestry Grant, 2005

Kim Reining-Gray, Science Department Chair/Teacher
Central High School
2155 Napier Avenue
Macon, Georgia 31204
School Telephone Number: (478) 751-6770
E-mail: kreining.central@bibb.k12.ga.us

Number of Years Teaching: 17
Awards: CIBA Specialty Chemicals Education Foundation,
NSTA Exemplary Science Teaching Award, High
School Level, 2005
Bibb County Board of Education "Beacon Light
Award," 2005
Georgia Science Teacher's Association, District VII
Secondary Teacher of the Year, 2004

Pam Roller, Second-Grade Teacher
Galveston Elementary
401 South Maple Street
Galveston, Indiana 46932
School Telephone Number: (574) 699-6687
E-mail: rollerp@sesc.k12.in.us

Number of Years Teaching: 32
Awards: Japan Fulbright Memorial Fund Teacher Participant,
2005
Disney American Teacher Awards Honoree, 2003

Jeff Shull, Chemistry and Physics Teacher, Department Chair
Macomb Academy of Arts and Sciences
23211 Prospect Street
Armada, Michigan 48005
School Telephone Number: (586) 784-9169 ext. 592
E-mail: jshull@armadaschools.org

Number of Years Teaching: 11
Award: National Science Teachers Association and Shell Oil
Company Science Teaching Award Semifinalist, 2005

Carol J. Skousen, Third-Grade Teacher, Science Specialist
Twin Peaks Elementary School
5325 South 1045 East
Murray, Utah 84117
School Telephone Number: (801) 646-5049
E-mail: carol.skousen@granite.k12.ut.us

Number of Years Teaching: 29
Awards: Glencoe Educator Award, 2005
Presidential Awards for Excellence in Mathematics
and Science Teaching, 2004
Utah's Region 6 Outstanding Elementary Science
Educator, 1998
Teacher of the Year, Twin Peaks Elementary School,
1995, 1996, 1997, 1998

Stanley A. Wawrzyniak, Science and Engineering Teacher
   Bow High School
   32 White Rock Hill Road
   Bow, New Hampshire 03304
   School Telephone Number: (603) 228-2210
   E-mail: swawrzyniak@bownet.org

   Number of Years Teaching: 21
   Awards: Vernier Technology Award, 2005
             Lemelson MIT InvenTeams Grants, 2002, 2004

Brenda Zabel, Science Department Chair
   Westside High School
   8701 Pacific Street
   Omaha, Nebraska 68114
   School Telephone Number: (402) 343-2732
   E-mail: brendazabel@westside66.org

   Number of Years Teaching: 20
   Awards: Nebraska Teacher of the Year, 2005
             Phi Delta Kappa Showcase Teacher, 2002

To friendship and to my friend Bev

CHAPTER 1

Expeditionary Learning Receives Prestigious Toyota Tapestry Grant

Project Dracula

Peter M. Menth

Rohnert Park, California

Mountain Shadows Middle School's Expeditionary Learning (Ex. L.) program has been awarded the prestigious Toyota Tapestry Grant to study bats in Sonoma County. The Toyota Corporation of America provides funding for innovative and creative approaches to science education, with the National Science Teachers Association (NSTA) administering the awards.

The grant competition was formidable, because NSTA received more than 500 applications from all over the United States, and Expeditionary Learning received one of only 50 $10,000 grant awards. Project Director and Ex. L. Science Teacher Peter Menthe was flown to the NSTA National Convention in Dallas to receive the award on behalf of Expeditionary Learning.

The project had to demonstrate adherence to California science education standards, involve the community at large, have an environmental component, exploit technology, and have the support of the school district. This grant is one of the many exciting and innovative ways that Mountain Shadows Middle School's Ex. L. program demonstrates to students the relevance of their education. The students and teachers of Ex. L. are well suited to the challenges of a project like this and are eager to begin.

Project Dracula, as it is known, seeks to improve the situation for local bat species. It is a well-known fact that bat populations are in severe decline. One of the reasons for this decline in our area is loss of habitat, specifically suitable bat roosting sites. It is the goal of Expeditionary Learning students and teachers to research the natural history of local bat species while attempting to dispel common misconceptions about bats. Students will use various survey techniques to determine population levels of a few species and construct and provide bat houses for roosting. Students will continue these surveys for a year or more to try to determine if bat populations have indeed risen as a result of increased suitable roosting sites.

In addition, with the cooperation of area farmers, the project is also intended to reduce the amount of insecticides applied to local agricultural fields. It has been documented that a single bat can consume from 300 to 1,000 insects in one night. If those insects are responsible for agricultural damage and if the number of insect-eating bats can be significantly increased, it is hoped that insecticide use in our area could be decreased. If local bat populations can be increased, thereby adding to the overall health of our local ecosystem, we hope that the need for insecticides can be reduced.

The students learn the use of state-of-the-art electronics and proper field research techniques. The grant funds the purchase of night-vision goggles, ultrasonic bat detectors and digital recorders, computers, and software to aid in data analysis and the identification of different bat species. Students will also be responsible for the construction, placement, and maintenance of many bat houses.

One of the places Ex. L. students monitor bats is at the Fairfield Osborne Preserve on Sonoma Mountain, which is overseen by Sonoma State University. This relatively unspoiled patch of oak woodland habitat with its diverse natural features is an ideal place to try to establish some baseline data for the project. The students try to locate other suitable sites around Rohnert Park to survey bats and to create a bat population database. Ex. L. students compile and analyze the data and draw conclusions based on their findings. The students are responsible for presenting their findings at various forums.

CHAPTER 2

Less Is More . . . Really

Stanley A. Wawrzyniak

Bow, New Hampshire

O ver the past 21 years of teaching science, I have worked increasingly hard to find, modify, and include hands-on, minds-on activities in my classes. When I was a first-year teacher, the activities were often limited to the chapter laboratory activities that came with the textbook series. I lectured from the text, and at the end of each chapter, students completed the chapter's lab activity. This was not the way I was taught to teach in my science teaching methods course at college, but as a first-year teacher, I felt overwhelmed. Even the good students seemed bored, and I knew the class would benefit from more hands-on activities.

I began collecting lab activities from dozens of text series and books of hands-on science activities. I modified the activities to emphasize observation, data collection, data analysis, conclusions, support for conclusions, and applications—the work that scientists do. My goal was and is to find activities for every major concept that students needed to learn. I wanted hands-on activities, not group lectures, to increasingly become the primary mode of instruction.

I also wanted each student to have a highly organized notebook that included all of his or her written work and all written course materials. Students received numbered pages, a few at a time, of what I called the study guide. The study guide for each class included directions for all activities. There were spaces for students to record observations, support conclusions, apply what they had learned, and answer questions.

There was no need for a separate notebook for notes. The class text was used as a resource to help answer questions and support conclusions. Years after completing my class, some students told me that they had kept and used their study guides in upper-level high school and even college courses. The students valued the study guides, because they were personal texts written in their own words. Even though my students and I felt that the study guide was a great way to organize course work, I was bothered by the fact that I never seemed to teach the entire curriculum. But in the days before widespread state testing, my supervisors and I didn't see this as a problem.

I realized years later that even though I was emphasizing hands-on activities, I was incorporating them into a traditional lecture format. Because the study guide directions I wrote for activities still needed clarification, I demonstrated them to the whole class before doing the activities. Even though I wanted the study guide activities to be the primary mode of instruction, I still felt obliged to summarize them to the whole class after completing them.

I thought that only my explanation, confirming what many of my students had already learned, would ensure learning. I believed that students who didn't really understand the activities would need my explanation the most. I wasn't delivering activity-based instructional materials that my students could use independently. Students who finished early needed to wait until their classmates caught up so we could talk about it together as a group.

I was experiencing the same problem faced by many of my colleagues. Hands-on science is time-consuming. It is easier to cover the entire curriculum if the number of hands-on activities is limited in favor of whole-group demonstrations and lectures. Learning outcomes are generally better for educationally sound hands-on activities than for whole-group activities, but there is not enough time to use them to teach everything. Science education reform seemed to promise less content material that could be learned by making use of time-consuming, hands-on activities involving observation and inquiry. I embraced this idea of "less is more." Current national and state science education expectations reflect science education reform, but the resulting quantity of science content is still sizable.

Six years ago, the way I taught changed forever and for the better. I began teaching classes from a national high school engineering program called Project Lead The Way (PLTW). I was impressed by the fact that the courses emphasized the hands-on application of math and science to solve problems. The course activities require students to use equipment and computer software and technology used by college-level engineering students and, in some cases, by engineers. I attended a two-week residential training program at the Rochester Institute of Technology to learn how to teach digital electronics (DE).

At the time, DE was one of five high school engineering courses developed by PLTW. I had taught basic electricity in science classes, but the extent of my knowledge was covered in the first few hours of training. I began teaching two sections of DE the following September. In addition to training, PLTW provides nearly all the curricular materials needed to teach their courses, including PowerPoint presentations for all major content, detailed directions for computer simulations and hands-on activities, unit quizzes and tests, and a variety of worksheets.

Schools that teach PLTW courses agree to purchase the software, equipment, and materials needed to teach the courses. At first, I was excited to be teaching a course for which I wouldn't have to write a comprehensive study guide and spend hours looking for activities and requesting the purchase of appropriate equipment and materials—as I did when teaching science.

During my first year teaching DE, I struggled with the content and made gradual progress, using the PLTW materials as I had learned at training. A short time after midterm exams, I began to think about the final exam. As with most PLTW courses, students who successfully complete the course are eligible to earn college credit from the

Rochester Institute of Technology (RIT) based on their scores on an RIT-prepared final exam. It was one of the major selling points for the engineering program at our school.

By my estimation, my class was a little more that one quarter of the way through the curriculum. Part of the problem was my inexperience with the course, but then again, I didn't have a great track record of teaching the entire curriculum for any course. Other teachers were successful. My DE students would not successfully complete the entire class and be prepared for the final exam unless I changed instruction methods significantly and immediately.

I still remember talking to that first class about the need to change instruction. Up to that point, instruction typically followed a pattern. Units began with introductory lectures including the use of PLTW PowerPoint presentations. I often demonstrated the circuit simulations to the whole class, making use of an LCD projector, because students couldn't always follow the PLTW directions.

At times, PLTW worksheets with directions for wiring actual circuits also needed to be clarified with the entire group. After students finished their work, the class met again as a whole group to discuss what happened and to explain why it happened. All the PLTW worksheets became part of each student's three-ring course binder. This basic cycle repeated itself with new course content. Before testing, there were whole-group reviews to make sure that everyone understood the material. It reminded me of an old saying that I vaguely connect with the military: Tell them what they need to do, have them do it, and tell them what they did.

I thought long and hard about where I could cut corners in instruction. At this time, I was still incorporating hands-on activities into a lecture format: Lecture before the activity about how to do it, do the activity, and lecture after the activity about what had happened. It seemed obvious to me that students needed to do the circuit simulations and circuit building. Half the credit for each unit exam and final exam was practical—simulating and building circuits.

I have always thought that the hands-on activities should be the primary method of learning course content. For the second half of the year, the circuit simulations and builds were emphasized, with little time for whole-group instruction. I believed that students would not get what I thought was the significant benefit from the whole-group lectures, discussions, and demonstrations. I felt bad, convinced that I would be limiting instruction.

I promised myself to do a better job of pacing the following year, when I was more familiar with the course material. The students took the news very well, and I spent much more time than usual working with students individually to clarify instructions and to answer questions. I still can't believe that I was so convinced that my lectures on the hands-on activities and related content were so critical.

The school year ended, and it was time for the final exam. I asked my students what they thought about the change to placing the emphasis on individual activities. A few casually mentioned that they did remember the course improving after midterm exams. The other students said that they really didn't notice that much of a change, but the course was okay. I graded the final exams, and my students did well. I felt that the test was a good representation of what students needed to know and to be able to do for the course. The students who did well throughout the course did well enough on the final exam to earn college credit.

The biggest problem for me is the amount of effort it takes to produce work guides that allow and require students to work independently. Most of the activities I find need to be modified for clarity, at minimum. Software and equipment change, and changes require revision of the work guides. New activities require new, detailed directions and testing to see if they work and if they help teach the content. Even room setups can be a problem.

Traditional classroom setups arrange desks facing the front of the room and the teacher. This can make it very difficult for the teacher to move around the room to work with individual students. All in all, I am encouraged by my classes and the support from teachers I work with—and by their use of work guides in their classes, to some extent. Less really can be more.

CHAPTER 3

More Than Just Rockets

Douglas L. Bailer
Hollywood, Alabama

Many science teachers appreciate the learning and excitement that come from the hands-on nature of building model rockets. Teachers know that there are many interesting scientific principles that can be demonstrated through model rocketry (laws of motion, simple aerodynamics, and more). Teachers also know that rockets are *fun,* and that fun can lead to enthusiasm and enthusiasm can lead to real learning. Basic model rockets, however, can be stepped up a notch by applying a couple of simple ideas.

First, unless you are teaching junior high students, prefabricated kits should be avoided. These kits include all the parts (nose cone, body tube, fins, and parachute) ready to be glued together. Instead, for high school students, teachers will find a higher level of student engagement through the use of bare-bones rocket sets. The best set I've found is marketed by Pitsco (http://www.shop-pitsco.com/) as the Economy Rocket Pack ($175 for 30 rockets).

With this pack, students are provided a strip of gummed paper with which they build their body tubes from scratch. The pack also includes a piece of material out of which students are to cut fins of their own design. Students must also cut out and string their own parachutes. The only pre-fabricated part provided is the nose cone. The use of a bare-bones rocket kit requires considerably more effort (and learning) on the part of the students.

Once students have mastered the basics by building their first model rockets, teachers can add to the learning by presenting the students with a modification challenge. The challenge should be based on the students' age and the time available. Challenges that I have used in the past include modifying the body tube to a longer length and determining the effect on the flight performance; constructing a nose cone that is capable of carrying an egg safely (small plastic soft drink bottles really work well as nose cones—provided the eggs are cushioned well); and testing the flight characteristics of the model with different fin configurations (altering the number of fins, the shape of fins, or the surface area of the fins). In any case, the modifications should be checked for safety before launch. Model rocket safety information is available from the National Association of Rocketry, http://www.nar.org/NARmrsc.html.

Helpful Tips

- The bare-bones kits will take considerably longer to complete compared to the prefabricated kits. I would allow four to five construction periods of about 20 to 30 minutes each. Don't scrunch this into one or two days—remember to allow for drying time between steps.
- Safety first! For teachers new to model rockets, remember that the kits produce disproportionately large amounts of flame when launched. Always ensure that students and flammable materials are an adequate distance from the launch zone.

■ Normally, when launching a model for the first time, you will want to start with the lowest-impulse engine available. When launching a rocket with a modified nose cone carrying an egg, however, this is not a good idea. Rocket stability is dependent upon the model reaching a minimum speed. (Airflow over the fins provides stabilization.) The heavier kits will require more force to reach the required speed—thus, a more powerful engine is desirable.

CHAPTER 4

Gravity

Carol J. Skousen

Murray, Utah

T he following activities align with Utah's Third-Grade Science Core Curriculum.

Activity One: Double Drop

Materials Needed

- One sturdy chair
- One piece of paper
- One golf ball
- One Ping-Pong ball
- Trade book: *Gravity Is a Mystery* by Franklyn M. Branley, illustrated by Don Madden, HarperCollins Children's Books (1986)

Directions

1. Begin by passing out the students' science journals for the Gravity Unit. The first page is a know/would like to know/learned (KWL)

chart. Instruct the students to write down everything they already *know* about gravity in the first column (K)—this task serves as a preassessment. Next, instruct the students to write anything they *would like to know* about gravity in the middle column (W). I remind the students that they may add questions to the middle column at any time during the unit.

2. Stand on a sturdy chair and hold up a flat piece of paper and a golf ball and ask, "Which will hit the floor first, if dropped from the same height and at the same time?" (The overwhelming response is that the ball will hit first because it weighs more.)

3. Release the two objects. (Sure enough, the ball hits first.)

4. Then, crumple the piece of paper tightly and repeat the experiment. (This time the two objects hit the floor at the same time.)

5. As a class, analyze the difference in the two experiments. Through discussion and probing questions, help the students to come to the conclusion that the ball hits first when the paper is flat because of air resistance. Make an analogy between the flat piece of paper and the way a parachute works.

6. Repeat the experiment one more time with a golf ball and a Ping-Pong ball.

7. As a class, discuss the results.

8. Read the trade book *Gravity Is a Mystery.*

9. Have the students write what they have *learned* about gravity in the L column on their KWL charts, and any new questions they have in the W column.

▨ Activity Two: Cup Catcher

Materials Needed

- One 7- or 8-ounce paper or plastic drinking cup, per student
- One 18-inch piece of string, per student

- One 6" × 6" piece of aluminum foil, per student
- One 1-inch piece of masking or Scotch tape, per student

Directions

1. Have each student construct his or her own cup catcher.
   a. Tape one end of the string to the middle of a 6" × 6" piece of aluminum foil.
   b. Crumple the foil into a tight round ball, leaving the loose end of string extending from the foil ball.
   c. Punch a hole in the cup near the lip of the cup.
   d. Tie the loose end of the string to the cup through the punched hole.

2. Have the students experiment with the cup catchers, observing how gravity is pulling the foil ball down toward the center of the earth—hopefully being caught in the cup.

3. Have the students write what they have *learned* about gravity in the L column on their KWL charts, and any new questions they have in the W column.

▨ Activity Three: Weighing Objects

Materials Needed

- Assorted classroom objects
- Spring scale (0–2,000 grams)

Directions

1. Estimate the order of the weight of various classroom objects, from lightest to heaviest.

2. Measure the weight of each object using the spring scale.

3. Compare the actual results with the estimates in Step 1.

4. Place the objects in the correct order from lightest to heaviest.

5. Have the students list the objects from lightest to heaviest in their journals, including the actual weight of each object.

6. Have the students write what they have *learned* about gravity in the L column on their KWL charts, and any new questions they have in the W column.

▧ Activity Four: Chair Jumping

Material Needed

- One sturdy chair

Directions

1. Review previous knowledge about gravity by playing Thumbs Up/Thumbs Down with true and false statements about gravity.

2. Place a sturdy chair in the front of the room.

3. Invite a student to stand on the seat of the chair.

4. Instruct the student to jump off the chair.

5. Instruct the student to jump back onto the seat of the chair.

6. Ask: "Which was easier—jumping off or jumping back onto the seat of the chair?"

7. Discuss as a class why it is easier to jump off. (The conclusion that should be reached is that gravity is helping to pull you down when you jump off the chair, but you are fighting against gravity when you jump back up onto the seat.)

8. Relate the results of the chair-jumping experiment to the real-life situation of riding a bike on a level surface, up an incline, and down a hill. Instruct the students that they are going to pantomime going on a bike ride and they need to listen carefully as you describe the terrain and respond appropriately.

9. Ask: "How did gravity affect your bike ride?" (The conclusion that should be reached is that gravity is helping to pull you down when you are riding downhill so you can coast. When you are riding uphill, you have to pedal harder because you are moving against the force of gravity.)

10. Have the students write what they have *learned* about gravity in the L column on their KWL charts, and any new questions they have in the W column.

▧ Activity Five: It's an Uphill Battle

Materials Needed

- Two chairs
- One pipe insulator (cut in half lengthwise)
- One marble
- Masking tape
- Yardstick
- Data recording sheet: It's an Uphill Battle

Directions

1. Place the chairs approximately 24 inches apart.

2. Place the pipe insulation between the two chairs, forming a U and extending 30 inches off the floor at both ends, while having the lowest part barely touching the floor. Tape the pipe insulation onto the chairs.

3. Explain to the students that you are going to release a marble from various starting points and they are going to predict how far up on the other side the marble will roll.

4. Place the marble on the pipe insulation 24 inches from the floor and release it. Observe how far up the other side the marble traveled. Record your observations on the It's an Uphill Battle data recording sheet.

5. Repeat Step 4 from the height of 18 inches, 12 inches, and 6 inches.

6. Analyze and discuss the results.

7. Have the students write what they have *learned* about gravity in the L column on their KWL charts, and any new questions they have in the W column.

Activity Six: Roller Coaster Fun

Materials Needed

- Video: *Roller Coaster!* (1993, WGBH Educational Foundation)
- One pipe insulator (cut in half lengthwise), per group
- Various 1-inch balls (such as steel, glass, cork, wood, rubber), per group
- Masking tape—one roll per group

Directions

1. Show a portion of the video *Roller Coaster!*

2. Divide the class into cooperative learning groups of four to five students per group.

3. Instruct the students that they are to design and construct a roller coaster by taping the pipe insulation onto the wall. They will need to analyze and modify their designs until they have built a roller coaster on which at least one of the five balls successfully completes the entire course of the track. Instruct the students to leave their successful designs taped to the wall.

4. When all the groups have constructed and built a successful roller coaster, have one group at a time share their final product. Discuss design problems and how they were solved. Ask: "Which balls worked the best and why?" Ask: "Which balls did not work and why?"

5. Have each student draw an illustration of his or her group's roller coaster in his or her science journal. Instruct each student to write about the activity, including problems encountered and modifications made to solve the problems. Also, have each student write about which balls were successful and which balls did not work and why.

6. Have the students write what they have *learned* about gravity in the L column on their KWL charts, and any new questions they have in the W column.

Activity Seven: Ball Throwing

Materials Needed

- Video: *Lift-Off to Learning,* Space Basics, produced by NASA
- Tennis ball, one per two students
- Overhead transparency: Throwing Balls

Directions

1. Display the Throwing Balls overhead transparency. Have the students predict which scenario is correct.

2. Watch a computer segment of the video *Lift-Off to Learning,* Space Basics.

3. Go outside and have the students experiment throwing a ball. Instruct the students to observe and analyze the forces acting on the ball and the results of these forces.

4. Have the students discuss and analyze the overhead transparency pictures again and reach a conclusion of what happens to a ball that is thrown into the air.

5. Have each student draw an illustration of throwing a ball in his or her journal, labeling the forces and the directions of the forces being applied to the thrown ball.

6. Have the students write what they have *learned* about gravity in the L column on their KWL charts, and any new questions they have in the W column.

▨ Activity Eight: Culminating/Home Connection

Material Needed

- Trade book: *The Gravity Company* by John B. Sandford, Abingdon Press (1988)

Directions

1. Challenge the students to design and make a paper airplane that will defy gravity by flying in the straightest and longest path.

2. Have the students bring their airplanes to school the next day for test flights.

3. Have one student at a time fly his or her airplane. This is best done in a hall with tile on the floor.

4. Record the results. To determine each student's result, count how many tiles out from the starting line the plane flew. Then, subtract the number of tiles off course (to the left or right).

5. Analyze which airplanes were the most successful in meeting the criteria and why. Discuss if there are some variables in the experiment that could possibly influence the results and how we could control those variables.

6. Have the students write what they have *learned* about gravity in the L column on their KWL charts, and any new questions they have in the W column.

7. If there's time, read the trade book *The Gravity Company* by John B. Sandford, Abingdon Press (1988), and discuss the errors.

Helpful Tips

- Prior to each activity, gather and ready all the materials needed.
- Use a variety of teaching strategies and resources.
- The needs of visual, auditory, and kinesthetic learning styles are met through charting data, creating illustrations, giving oral presentations, singing songs, and participating in hands-on activities.
- When grouping the students, keep in mind the diverse needs and ability of each student. The groups work best when there is a mixture of abilities. English-as-a-second-language (ESL) students are placed with students who act as mentors.
- Small groups of four to five allow all students to participate fully in accomplishing the task and aid one another in understanding the concept.
- Give unsuccessful groups extra time to make modifications, as well as suggestions from the rest of the class.
- Though the use of five different balls for the Roller Coaster Fun Activity is not necessary to learn the targeted concept, the five balls make the activity more interesting and add a challenge for the brighter students.
- I teach this unit over a period of one week:

  Day One. Activity One: Double Drop and Activity Two: Cup Catcher

  Day Two. Activity Three: Weighing Objects

  Day Three. Activity Four: Chair Jumping, Activity Five: It's an Uphill Battle, and Activity Six: Roller Coaster Fun

  Day Four. Activity Seven: Ball Throwing. Assign homework: Making paper airplanes

  Day Five. Activity Eight: Culminating/Home Connection

CHAPTER 5

Making Microbes Fun

Jason E. Hughes

Ravenswood, West Virginia

T eaching students about microorganisms can be challenging, and learning about microorganisms can be boring to students. Without enjoyable, engaging, and relevant lessons and labs, students will lose interest in the subject very fast. As a follow-up to a lesson on the different types of microorganisms—bacteria, protozoa, fungi, algae, and viruses—I conduct a lab activity that all the students seem to enjoy, the entire class is engaged, and the students have a sincere interest in the outcome of the lab.

The class is divided into teams of two and three and then told that they are "microbe detectives." Each team of detectives is given some Q-tips and a Petri dish of nutrient agar. The assignment is to go through the school building swabbing as many places as possible that the students think would be sources of microorganisms. Students take samples from water fountains, cafeteria tables, lockers, locker room floors, doorknobs, trash cans, teacher desks, and commode seats. I accompany them as they go through the school to make sure that they do not interrupt other classrooms. I try to create the feeling that we are sneaking through the school to take the samples.

The samples are returned to the lab and placed in an incubator. If an incubator is not available, setting the samples out at room temperature will also work. The Petri dishes are observed for the next few days. Generally, bacterial and fungal growth can be observed after 24 hours. The students are asked to identify what they observe. Bacteria are generally slimy in appearance, and fungi are generally fuzzy. The students are immediately able to see microbe growth from the different areas around the school. Of course, many of the students gasp when they see what was growing in their lockers or on the water fountain handle!

After day three, we conduct another lab experiment with the samples taken from around the school. We conduct a gram staining lab of the bacteria. The gram staining experiment involves taking a sample of bacteria from the Petri dish using an inoculating loop and mixing it with a drop of water on a microscope slide. The slide is then passed through an open flame to fix the slide.

The slide then goes through a three-step procedure of staining. After staining the sample, the students use a microscope with an oil immersion lens to observe the bacteria. The students write down the different bacteria shapes that they observe and whether the bacteria are gram-positive (purple color and susceptible to antibiotics) or gram-negative (pink color and not susceptible to antibiotics).

Through this multiday and multilab activity, students gain many valuable skills and learn a great deal about the microscopic world around them. The students learn the importance of teamwork while working with partners through the entire process. They learn that there are microbes all around us and that some are harmful, but many are harmless or beneficial. Many of the students take hand washing more seriously after this activity. Most of all, the students realize that science can be fun.

Helpful Tips

- All the supplies mentioned for this activity can be obtained from most scientific supply companies.

- One of the great things about this activity is that I never have any discipline problems. The students are actively engaged throughout the process. Some students may get a little loud in the hallways, but if you suggest to them that the entire process of collecting samples in the school is a secret and that they are not to get caught, I believe most students will remain quiet. It is also a good idea to inform the other teachers and administrators about the activity going on that day.

CHAPTER 6

Building Our Curriculum as We Build a Straw-Bale Greenhouse

Sally Ogilvie

Syracuse, Utah

S yracuse Elementary School is located in northern Utah in a farming community experiencing a great deal of suburban sprawl. Many of our 950 students come from a farming background. Our community, anxious to preserve this agricultural heritage, supports our quarter-acre outdoor school garden with adult and student volunteer service. Community members and our school staff formed a committee under my direction to build an environmentally friendly and innovative straw-bale greenhouse/learning center to extend educational opportunities in our garden. The 15-foot × 25-foot building was built in 2006 with community donations of labor and grant monies.

Our building project involved every grade level in both the design and building phases of this project. Students used geometry and math to measure and problem-solve the building design; utilized scientific processes to understand the solar power and energy needed to create an optimal growing environment in the greenhouse; developed plant experiments to understand the benefits of greenhouse biology; and designed models to illustrate concepts of physical science. Our greenhouse project connects real-life work to curriculum goals and promotes experimental science and math.

After the foundation was poured and the building framed, a straw-bale workshop of nine participants paid tuition to learn the techniques of straw-bale and earthen plaster building. The participants built the straw walls, reinforcing them with 8-foot bamboo poles. They applied four coats of earthen plaster to the exterior and interior walls. During the workshop, kindergarten through sixth-grade students sifted soil; mixed the plaster of soil, straw, and water; and helped apply the plaster to the walls with adult supervision.

Our completed greenhouse has polycarbonate sheets and windows to bring in natural light. It is also equipped with two roof turbines for humidity control, as well as electricity, culinary water, and lights. Students decorated the walls using 4-inch tiles they painted and inserted into the final coat of earthen plaster. Community members molded large insects out of earthen plaster for the walls of our greenhouse.

Each grade level at our elementary school is in charge of a specific section of our garden. The greenhouse will support their stewardship with seed propagation, pollination, soil studies, insect control experiments, as well as sustainable agriculture and nutrition as part of a healthy lifestyle for our young students. Teachers will connect these areas with curriculum in science, math, social studies, art, and community service.

Our 5-year goal is for our greenhouse to be financially self-sufficient by 2011. Students plan to sell our seedlings, plants, and vegetables during the school year to augment the greenhouse budget. Hopefully, produce from our garden will support our lunchroom as well. This project has been a large goal to complete. However, teachers, community members, and students have gained confidence that we can build a house using renewable, sustainable, and environmentally responsible technology . . . all by ourselves!

Helpful Tips

- I underestimated how much money the greenhouse would cost. Our building committee wrote grant proposals and held fundraisers to help with the costs. We still had to spend personal funds to complete the project.
- It is imperative to have architectural support and consultants who are knowledgeable about straw-bale building. Be sure to involve students in the building process. The ownership they derive from being included in each step of erecting the building creates hands-on learning opportunities and helps with vandalism control. I wouldn't attempt this project without a supportive principal, staff, and community behind you. They will help you when the project runs into snags and cheer you on with your successes. It is a *big* project...but I have found it to be worthwhile both academically and in terms of service learning for all.

CHAPTER 7

Real-World Science Engagement

Kim Reining-Gray

Macon, Georgia

Teaching science has changed considerably over my 17-year career. Today's students want action, application, and relevance in their academic endeavors. Woe is the teacher who cannot keep the attention of a 15-year-old high school student in today's public schools. In an effort to keep pace with my students, I assign practical problems that require their creativity and critical thinking to solve.

Superstar Shoes: We Got Shoes if You Got Game!

One example is "Superstar Shoes." Prior to giving the students this memo, I have taught the concepts of friction, weight and mass, and coefficient of friction. They engage in a lab activity investigating the different forces needed to pull an object across various types of surfaces to discover that the weight of the object and the surface are what determine the coefficient of friction, or the "grab" the two objects have between them.

I have used this lab with all levels of students. I make adjustments for struggling students and give very little assistance to my gifted students. I require all students to write a formal report, including all steps of the scientific method to be submitted to the "sales department manager."

Memo: Shoe Sales

To: Research & Development

From: Sales Department Manager, Seymour Sales

Dear R & D Department,

We have learned from our marketing associates that our number one competitor, Sole Shoes, is about to corner the market on basketball performance footwear. They have modified the sole of their current athletic shoe to make it "grab" the court better. We all know that the less time on your butt and the more time on your feet, the higher the score will be! Our company must quickly research different types of shoe soles to determine which one will have the most "grab" (friction) on the basketball court.

Please conduct the necessary research and send me your report no later than _____. The progress and growth of our company are in your hands, or rather, your feet!

Respectfully,

Seymour Sales

Scientific Method for Reluctant Scientists

As science teachers, we stress the scientific method, but we seldom assist students with a good science fair project. There are so many other demands during the school day that science investigation has fallen by the wayside. To combat my students' lack of experience and understanding, I often assign a group project with some guidance.

One investigation allows students to determine the safety of the school. I presented my students with this problem, and they brainstormed various tests to perform. The class divided into small groups, and each group investigated a unique safety concern of our school. Some of their ideas included handicapped access, water and air quality, noise pollution, temperature control of cafeteria food, and lighting adequacy.

Each group collected data by visiting sites in the school and making observations. Students asked to use light meters, digital temperature probes, microphones, and water and air test kits. The group investigating the handicapped access contacted the local planning and zoning board to determine the current requirements for rise and run of stairs and ramps. They then measured our facilities to determine adequacy. All groups took digital photos of their work in progress.

After collecting data, each group was required to present its investigation and its data analysis and results to the class through a PowerPoint presentation. On the day of presentations, local school board personnel and representatives were invited, as were faculty, to learn about the safety of our school. Students were surprised to learn that our school is safe, and they thoroughly enjoyed presenting for an audience. I highly recommend projects like this one to engage students in the investigative process as well as creative presentation and public speaking.

Build a Science Community

As a science educator, one of my main goals is to promote scientific investigation and critical thinking. So many elementary teachers are swamped with reading, writing, and math that science often takes a backseat. To help elementary teachers and their students experience science, I use my high school students as experts. I usually coordinate a project with another teacher—biology and physical sciences work well together. We divide our students into small groups and assign the task of "teaching" a concept to an elementary group. Our students have the freedom of selecting the topic and their method of instruction. We require only teacher approval. We help our students find information, develop activities, and fine-tune their delivery.

During the spring, we choose one day to either have our students visit the elementary school or to have all students go to the local park. Our high schoolers set up mini-stations of science investigations and experiments for the elementary students. The elementary students go from station to station to have a day of "hands-on science."

This has been a big hit with both older and younger students. The elementary teachers appreciate the effort, and we are hopeful that the Criterion-Referenced Competency Test (CRCT) scores will reflect this intense science review. Our older students enjoy the opportunity to be experts, and they work exceptionally well with the younger kids. The planning on the front end of this activity is huge. It is difficult to coordinate so many kids, find a place to meet, design the activities, and still cover the required curriculum. The advantages, however, far outweigh the headaches. Elementary schools call me early in the year to ask to be our target school for the project. Using this activity strengthens both our school community and our science program.

What's in a Cheeto?

This lab is a spin-off of the traditional "burn a Cheeto" lab. My students investigate the specific heat of a sample of metal prior to this lab so that they know the general plan for determining the energy of a substance. I distribute the Food and Drug Administration (FDA) lab, and we brainstorm about how to solve the problem. My students choose to burn the Cheeto to heat up a known mass of water while recording the change in temperature. They determine the number of calories per gram, and then they determine the percent error from the accepted caloric value on the Cheetos bag. This lab is a big hit!

Food and Drug Administration

To: Food Production Companies, Cheeto Division

Re: New Federal Food Guidelines

To Whom It May Concern:

The FDA has recently implemented new food nutrition label guidelines for all foods manufactured for human consumption. All foods must be retested for calorie content to maintain the continued sales of the product. A full analysis report is due to the FDA no later than _____. Be sure to include the following clearly labeled:

> Purpose
>
> Background Info
>
> Hypothesis
>
> Experimental Procedure (including variables and data collection)
>
> Data Analysis (percent error)
>
> Conclusion

Please follow the approved federal lab report guidelines in your manual.

Kim Reining-Gray

FDA Consumer Division

CHAPTER 8

A Method for Inquiry Science

Mark Goldner

Brookline, Massachusetts

My goal is that my students will become good scientific thinkers who have a deep understanding of key scientific concepts. Good scientific thinking means being able to generate questions for inquiry, develop sound hypotheses, design controlled experiments, collect and present appropriate data, use evidence to support a conclusion, and effectively communicate an experimental process.

In order to meet this goal, I have employed a method of inquiry science organized around students asking their own inquiry questions. Each investigation begins with a hands-on experience that is tied to the content of the unit, which then helps students generate questions, create hypotheses, and design and carry out experiments.

I am working to put in at least one inquiry investigation into each unit of the seventh- and eighth-grade curricula. In each case, I use the same general approach. First, in order to generate good questions around which to design an experiment, students must be given an initial experience that will lead to good inquiry questions.

As students are exploring the initial experience, they are also making lists of questions as a group. Students then work on turning their questions into what we call "investigable questions"—those questions that will lead to a controlled experiment. Lists of investigable questions are generated, students are grouped according to interest, and each group chooses an investigable question to study. Students then come up with a hypothesis that predicts the answer to their investigable question and they design an experiment to test their hypothesis. Once it is designed, the experiment proceeds and students collect data. Students then present their findings to the class.

After the presentations, I generally take the opportunity to do some directed teaching. My lesson is centered around the findings of the class, and if I have designed the initial experience properly and helped coach the students well through the process, then what I planned to teach has either (1) been "discovered" by the kids, or (2) they have raised questions leading directly to the content of my lesson.

Inevitably, however, some students have come across an observation that is new for me or questions I haven't thought of before! In my lesson, I take care to use examples from the students' experiments to illustrate the general scientific principles. Finally, I have the students write up the experience in a formal lab report, during which they are asked to make the connection between the data they collected and the general scientific principles we have discussed.

I have developed at least eight inquiry investigations. Following are three examples.

▧ Example 1: Microbes in a Jar Investigation

(Classification Unit: Seventh Grade)

Students create and observe a grass infusion (cut grass and water in a small sealed jar) over several days using a microscope. They develop investigable questions to explore with regard to the appearance of microorganisms and how changing their environment will change what they observe. Students create a hypothesis and design and carry out experiments.

Student questions lead to lessons on traditional classification schemes. Having gone through the inquiry experience gives kids a "need to know." They become interested in understanding why some of the organisms are classified as protists, some as bacteria, and still others as small animals. As they try to identify the microbes in their experiments, the students discover a need to know how to measure the sizes of objects under a microscope.

Doing this inquiry investigation has improved students' understanding of taxonomic schemes and how to use them. I have found much more interest in identification of organisms as they begin to see why identification is valuable. On follow-up activities and tests, students perform much better.

Example 2: Vacuum Investigation

(Properties of Matter Unit: Eighth Grade)

During this unit, students learn about kinetic molecular theory as it applies to different states of matter. Students also study, on a basic level, the relationships among temperature, volume, and pressure of a gas. I do a series of demonstrations for the students, using a bell jar and a small vacuum pump. Students then generate inquiry questions, develop hypotheses, and design short experiments (to be carried out under reduced pressure). Students collect data and present their findings, and I use their experiences to help make connections among kinetic theory, energy, and states of matter.

After going through this investigation, students show a deeper understanding of gas laws. On an in-class test, the students are asked to make predictions about the behavior of a gas given changes in the environment. I have seen an improvement in student performance on these questions. Students are also making connections between the experiments we did in class and situations in their own lives involving gases and changes of state.

▧ Example 3: Pollution Investigation

(Ecology Unit: Seventh Grade)

During the ecology unit, students are exposed to a variety of experiences highlighting ways that they contribute to local pollution. Students are challenged to think of ways that various types of pollution could be effectively modeled in the classroom (such as creating a miniature greenhouse, using household chemicals to simulate acid rain on plants, and creating simple particulate detectors for air pollution monitoring).

They generate investigable questions, develop hypotheses, and design experiments. During and after data collection, students are challenged to think about the limitations of their models and to connect their experiment with other background information gathered by scientists. Their findings are later incorporated into a "public service announcement" video project about types of pollution. (I am in discussion with Brookline Access TV to try to air the videos publicly.)

Having gone through an inquiry investigation around a real-life issue, students seem to feel a greater ownership of the issue. They are also able to make connections between science concepts and the effects of pollution. For example, in their public service videos, most students made strong connections between different types of pollution and disruption of the nutrient cycles. Such connections are a direct result of having gone through this investigation.

CHAPTER 9

Using Technology and Music to Motivate Science Students

Brenda Zabel

Omaha, Nebraska

I am fortunate to have many technology tools available as I teach my classes. My zoology/physiology teaching team members and I incorporate the materials we present to students into PowerPoint presentations. More than just text on slides, these presentations include music, still graphics, animations, and live video clips so that students can experience new information in a variety of sensory modalities. These multimedia tools make complex scientific phenomena like nerve impulse transmission easy to visualize and comprehend.

Among the many multimedia tools I use in my class, students report that music and humor best help them understand concepts. Every unit I teach begins with a song that is related to the content. In zoology, "Crocodile Rock" recorded by Elton John introduces reptiles, and "Rockin' Robin" recorded by Bobby Day introduces birds. In physiology, Frank Sinatra's "I've Got You Under My Skin" introduces epithelial tissue, while "Every Breath You Take" recorded by The Police leads off our study of the respiratory system. When students realize the connection between a popular song and what we're studying in class, they make important learning connections in a nontraditional way.

Another key technology component of our zoology/physiology course is our online support site, created using www.blackboard.com. My teaching colleagues and I expand and update our site each semester. Announcements, important documents, assignments, PDF versions of PowerPoint presentations, videos, lecture notes, and practice assessments support every aspect of our course. Video tutorials on a streaming server let students replicate and review the lab activities they've done in the classroom.

Posted assignments can be printed and completed in a traditional way, or they can be completed electronically, thus allowing students to pace their own work, collaborate with others, and revise as often as they wish before pressing the Send button. A discussion board provides "virtual office hours." Students may electronically post comments and questions, and classmates and I can respond to their postings wherever we are. It is not unusual for students to post up to 20 messages on the discussion board the evening before a major exam!

Students also contribute Web links to outside resources they find while doing independent research. Instructors and students benefit from these resources. Because all these support materials are Web based, students may access them 24 hours a day, 7 days a week, and anywhere they have Internet access.

Helpful Tip

- One thing I've learned is that students love to see their own ideas incorporated into teaching presentations. High school students, of course, also typically *love* popular music. My colleagues and I welcome student suggestions for songs the students feel are related to the topics we discuss in class. However, I've learned to screen the lyrics of these songs very carefully to avoid some potentially explicit moments in the classroom! Students don't care what we know until they know that we care!

CHAPTER 10

The Power of Building a Positive Classroom Climate

Cindy Corlett

Parker, Colorado

Think back to when you were a student. What was your favorite class? Who was your favorite teacher? Most likely, they were one and the same! It is no coincidence that you enjoy a subject area more when you feel a connection to the teacher. Effective teachers are purposeful about earning respect rather than expecting respect. Effective teachers learn about their students and find positive ways to highlight the uniqueness of each individual. Effective teachers understand that *students don't care what we know until they know that we care.*

One of the most effective ways to become a successful educator is to become a student of your students! Study them, and know who they are, what they like, and what they don't like. Find out what's important. Discover what makes them tick. Find out about family, friends, sports, pets, and activities. The more you know, the better equipped you are to meet their individual needs. The more you know and care, the more they will learn and care!

The importance of establishing a positive classroom culture and a climate of trust cannot be underestimated. Work to make your classroom a place where students want to be. Show students that you care about them. When teachers are positive and caring, students will trust and follow their leadership. Students are also more likely to accept consequences for their behavior from a teacher they trust and respect.

To gain respect, one must give it. This may not be the most creative idea in teaching—however, it is one of the most important. At some point during their careers, all effective and successful teachers realize the importance of building rapport and of positive classroom management. No matter the content area, students must *know that we care before they care what we know.* We must relate to them as people. One of the important needs of every student is the need to feel important. Students (and all humans!) want to be appreciated for all the positive things they can contribute.

Be a role model for students, even during the discipline process. Remember—we are the adults, they are the students. Though my desire is always to focus on the positive, I think it is worth mentioning some techniques that do *not* work. Unfortunately, in times of frustration, teachers sometimes resort to these techniques. Avoid raising your voice, using sarcasm or humiliation, drawing unrelated persons into the conflict, having a double standard (making students "do what I say, not what I do"), preaching, pleading, bribing, bringing up unrelated events, generalizing about students by making remarks such as "all you kids are the same," or holding grudges. Sometimes teachers will fall into negative discipline when frustrated or at a loss for effective strategies. A toolbox containing effective strategies will help teachers avoid these pitfalls.

Best practices for building rapport with students include the following: Assume a positive intent, be as fair as possible with all students, try to see the situation through the eyes of the students, allow students to save face and to maintain dignity at all times, and provide choices that allow for a win-win situation.

Modeling is also an important consideration. Observant eyes are always upon teachers. Students see us as examples of behavior. Like it or not, educators are role models. "Values are caught, not taught" is another adage to keep in mind. Teachers who are courteous, prompt, enthusiastic, in control, patient, and organized provide examples for their students through their own behavior. The "do as I say, not as I do" teachers send mixed messages that confuse students and invite disrespect and misbehavior.

Find what works for you and your students. *Meet and greet.* Meet students at the door. Greet them as they enter. This allows for personal contact with *every student, every day!* To get students in the mindset of science, I meet them at the door with a fun fact, an amusing joke (they often call them "groaners"), an artifact or sample, or sometimes even a cheer (T-E-S-T, time to show your B-E-S-T!). We greet each other with a smile. It is amazing what a positive tone this sets for our time together. Students will often come to the door and wait their turn to tell me a joke or a fact for the day. It has become such a norm for our classroom that on the rare occasions when I am not at the door, students come into the room concerned that I might be gone for the day.

Constant monitoring of student interaction and behavior is another valuable technique for success. The key to monitoring is to circulate. Get up and get around the room. Keep moving! While your students are working, make the rounds. Check on their progress. Interact with your students. An effective teacher makes a pass through the whole room within a few minutes after students have started an assignment, and many times throughout the class period. I am on my feet so often that students express shock on the rare occasions when I do sit. I have to say that with the constant monitoring, I sleep well at night!

Emphasize and reinforce positive behavior. Use classroom rules that describe the behaviors you want, instead of listing things the students cannot or should not do. Let your students know that this is how you expect them to behave in your classroom. Be clear on expectations and always model what you expect to see. Make ample use of praise. When you see good behavior, acknowledge it. Be *positive!*

Be creative. Be flexible. Find unique ways to build rapport and to maintain positive classroom management. Find what works for you . . . and for your students. Let students share in the responsibility of creating a positive climate within the classroom. Positive acknowledgment in the form of postcards, notes, phone calls home, and so on does wonders for the culture of the class. Emphasize the positive and diminish the negative. Let students "overhear" positive teacher talk. Praise publicly, redirect privately. Actively build a sense of community and belonging for all students.

Find best practices for positive rapport building and classroom management by seeking experts in your building. There are also many great books available. I recommend *First Days of School* by Harry Wong, *Winning Strategies for Classroom Management* by Carol Cummings, *Day One and Beyond* by Rick Wormelli, and *Classroom Management That Works* by Robert Marzano.

Every effective and successful teacher has an individual style. Create your own by using techniques that work for you. Successfully link elements from various sources to create your own best style and then continuously work to enhance your repertoire. Find ways for *every* student to be successful, and you in turn will be successful.

The old adage *"Students don't care what we know until they know that we care"* still holds true. Let it guide your practice.

CHAPTER 11

Mission Possible

Pam Roller

Galveston, Indiana

I t is my mission in life to give my students as many experiences as possible to stimulate and motivate them to want to learn. One of those experiences is what I call Mission Possible, and it is how I keep science alive in my class. I have had a space shuttle simulator in my classroom since 1996. It is 16 feet long, 8 feet high, and 8 feet wide. The mockup is a replica of the space shuttle, and it is fully equipped with computers, two-way cameras and radios, color TVs, and a VCR. I also have a mission control area in my classroom so the simulation can be as realistic as possible.

My second graders and their parents have had the opportunity to simulate missions in space through my School On Saturday Program. The program is offered to my second graders and their parents. It allows parents the opportunity to be engaged in a fun learning experience with their children. They actually suit up like astronauts and go through an actual launch, do orbital experiments, and end with a landing. The simulation is perfect for students to develop skills in problem solving and decision making and to learn the importance of cooperation and teamwork.

During the orbital part of the mission, my students have numerous opportunities to explore and make new discoveries as they conduct their own experiments growing plants and crystals. The students learn about responsibility and ownership when caring for their own plants. They have many opportunities to make observations, record data, infer, inquire, compare, and draw conclusions.

I recall one very memorable Mission Possible. It was during a School On Saturday Program with my second graders and their parents. This particular Saturday, the mother of one of my students was battling cancer and could not attend, so the student's grandmother, who has multiple sclerosis (MS) really badly, brought her to school so she could participate in Mission Possible. The grandmother could hardly get around but never complained. She had the best attitude and the most energy of anyone in attendance.

This grandmother suited up like everyone else and did all the experiments with enthusiasm beyond belief! After the mission, I told her what an inspiration she was! She said she decided to bring her granddaughter to simulate Mission Possible so she would be busy learning in a fun way and for a brief while she wouldn't be so worried about her mother. Not only are missions possible, anything is possible when you believe! The girl's mother is free from cancer and the grandmother still has MS but is still going strong!

I have offered my Mission Possible space shuttle simulation to the students in my afterschool Young Astronauts Program and to 22 different schools in Indiana through a Kids College Program offered at Indiana University Kokomo (IUK) in Kokomo, Indiana. Mission Possible was the name of a class I taught for Purdue University's summer institute for gifted students, which culminated with a field trip to my classroom to simulate a day mission. My class at Purdue University gave students from nine states and a student from Korea the opportunity to experience Mission Possible.

I attended Space Camp for Professional Educators in 1988 and have tried my best to keep the dream alive in my classroom. Because I am a lifelong learner and choose to fully engage myself in some kind of learning all the time, new opportunities happen continually. From my space camp experience, I started my own Young Astronauts Program in 1988 and it is still successful today. It is now a districtwide program.

Children are fascinated by space exploration. As a teacher, I think like a kid and use space as a way to hook my students' interest to get them to learn beyond what is required. My space experiences haven't stopped there. I have traveled to Russia twice to tour their space facilities and have met 12 U.S. astronauts and 2 cosmonaut trainees. My first trip to Russia was in June of 1991. I collaborated with a professor at the University of Alabama in Huntsville to bring one of the Russian cosmonaut trainees—who just happened to be in Huntsville in November for a space summit conference—to visit my school and community. The university freed him up, and my Young Astronauts sold enough 50-cent candy bars to pay for his flight from Alabama to Indiana. It was an awesome experience for our whole community.

My Young Astronauts had just built a life-size mockup of a space station. Yes, the students built it. As a matter of fact, the girls and boys were fighting over the electric screwdrivers used to assemble the station. The local newspaper took a photo of the students with the cosmonaut in front of the space station. He was welcomed and spoke at a whole-school assembly, and then he was shared with four school corporations.

I have coordinated the efforts so that my school and community could meet four different astronauts. Each visit was exciting and unique. One astronaut was a mission specialist and an author, one was a payload specialist, one was the pilot and later the commander of the space shuttle, and one was an astronaut during the Apollo era.

Helpful Tip

- Lifelong learning and worldwide travel are ongoing missions in my life. They enrich and enhance experiences in my classroom. Accepting challenges and taking risks keep me stimulated and motivated. Ultimately my students reap the benefits of having a teacher who allows her students many opportunities to apply what they are learning to real-life situations. Mission Possible was an unforgettable experience for many students. One student summed up his mission experience by saying that Mission Possible was on his list of top 10 field trips.

CHAPTER *12*

Robots

From Science Fiction to Science Fact

Lindsey Prentice

Evansville, Indiana

E vansville Lutheran School's fifth-grade class has been given a mission to design, build, and program a robot that will explore Mars. These robots will never actually see the surface of Mars, but through the course of the projects, the students will learn a little about Mars and see that robots are not just characters in science fiction but useful tools for science.

We began by first looking at science fiction literature with robots as characters within the story. This year we read *Orvis* by H. M. Hoover. As we read, we looked at the uses of the robots within the story, as well as comparing these uses to present-day machines that perform the same or similar functions. Our discussion led to topics of form versus function, human behavior in robots, and the usefulness of such things in our lives. Once done with this, we moved on to Part 2.

We looked in more detail at robots in modern life. To fully appreciate where we are now, we looked at the history and development of robots throughout our history. As a reference during this study, the students used the book *How to Build a Robot* by Clive Gifford. This is a great book that looks at the history and applications of robots. The book includes side projects that the students can do as well. Finally we moved on to Part 3, application. For most of the students, this is what they were waiting for: getting a chance to play with LEGOs.

To start off, I divided the class into Mission Teams consisting of four members, each with a specific job. All four members of the team worked together on the overall outcome of their missions, but each had a specific responsibility in the project. There was the Mission Leader, who made sure the group stayed on task and made sure everyone had something to work on. The Programmer was responsible for creating and giving the commands to run their robot. The Engineer led the design and building of the robot. And finally, the Data Analyzer took the data and information collected from each mission and put it together to display and share with the class.

For this part of the project, I used a curriculum and LEGO kits that LEGO Education and For Inspiration and Recognition of Science and Technology (FIRST) have already put together, "RoboChallenge: Exploration Mars." Through this curriculum, I can integrate what had been discussed in our literature reading with a "right-now" application. The students also expanded their knowledge of Mars as they researched information about the Red Planet that would be useful and beneficial in the design and programming of their robots. Within their teams, they saw the usefulness of robots within the science field as they collected and analyzed data and navigated obstacles with the robot that they had built from LEGO bricks and programmed with the school computer.

The fifth-grade class started with some "basic training" of the LEGO parts and the programming software before going into the specific missions. The programming sounded difficult to the students, but it was relatively simple with the software they used. The students used a program called RoboLab, which uses pictures or icons that represent actions they wanted the robot to do or how they wanted it to react. With instructions and practice, RoboLab was quite easy for the students to use.

After the completion of this training, each team received a kit with the same selection of LEGO parts and sensors. At this point, the teams began designing to meet the challenges of each mission, such as maneuvering through obstacles or having their robot run through a specific set of routines successfully.

This program was implemented to help incorporate more science fiction into our reading curriculum as well as to give our students a way to learn that is hands-on, creative, challenging, and simply fun.

Helpful Tips

- Make sure that the groups stay on task and have specific goals to reach at the end of each class period.
- This project is also a good opportunity to reinforce the concept of simple machines. After the project, if time permits, run a Robot Olympics in which the teams design, build, and program robots to compete in events, such as speed races or being able to knock over the most pillars in an allotted time period.

CHAPTER 13

A Different Kind of Service

Deborah Perryman

Elgin, Illinois

I have had many opportunities to ask people across the nation one very important question: "What do our students need from our schools?" A variety of answers have been given, some of which include understanding, support, an education, the ability to act as a citizen, and real-world problem-solving skills. The one response I have yet to be given is: "Our students need to be able to pass a state standardized test!" (Oddly, I have asked several legislatures this same question, and they never think of standardized tests either.)

We understand that the aforementioned are of great importance but are difficult to measure. Further, if we were to research the mission statements of schools across the nation, we would find some mention of "creating citizens." But when do our schools actually provide students with the opportunity to act as citizens? No Child Left Behind (NCLB) dictates that educators must help students meet or exceed state standards. This is certainly a worthy goal, as citizens must be educated and motivated to participate in society. Why not use the time we have in schools to actually show our young people how each state's learning standards will actually apply to their lives? Why not allow our students to solve community problems and act as citizens! I have found a teaching strategy that allows me to fold learning standards into community action. This strategy is called "service learning."

What Is Service Learning?

Service learning is a teaching strategy in which students explore an aspect of a community issue. The teacher works to tie the exploration into a project that addresses the curriculum (i.e., state standards). For example, picking up litter near a creek on a monthly basis can be related to the Clean Water Act and therefore fits my environmental curriculum. The students are exploring a community issue (i.e., litter and its effect on creeks) while meeting state learning standards (mandated by federal legislation). My long-term goal as their teacher may be for them to find the source of that litter and perhaps outline a permanent solution to the litter problem.

Service learning is *not* a stand-alone course; it is a teaching strategy that allows you to connect a student to the real-world pragmatism of your curriculum. Are you tired of students asking you: "When will I ever use this in the real world?" Help students make this connection by allowing them to solve those problems facing your community.

Service learning is *not* community service. Although community service projects are wonderful and do provide positive student outcomes, they are not tied directly to curriculum. Take as an example one of America's most popular community service projects, the canned food drive. Please tell me how placing collection boxes in a central location helps students meet state learning standards. Think for a moment how this community service project can be tweaked into a service learning project.

First, have you ever looked at what is collected? Are the items collected really needed in food banks? Why not have the students work with the food bank and find out what is really *needed* by its patrons? Students could create graphics clearly depicting their research and create a public outreach campaign to help the community get a better handle on the issue of hunger. Students could study why so many families are in need of the food bank. Why not have the students write press releases and articles for the local paper explaining the community need? The bottom line is that service learning is cross-curricular and makes a greater impact on our youth!

▧ Why Service Learning?

You only have to look at the National Training Laboratories Learning Pyramid for Average Retention Rates to understand the need to incorporate service learning into our schools. According to the Learning Pyramid, students retain 5 percent of what you tell them, 10 percent from what they read, 30 percent from audiovisual sources, 30 percent through demonstration, 40 percent from discussion groups, 75 percent from practice by doing, and 90 percent by teaching others. I utilize service learning because it emphasizes the last four teaching strategies mentioned in the pyramid. My own experience has shown me that the last statistic, "teaching others," is accurate. Think about everything you have learned in your curricular area throughout your career as a teacher. That marks an incredible learning curve. So why not involve students in teaching?

There are two other dimensions to service learning that are important to explore: reflection and community impact. First, studies have shown that reflection is the key to a well-designed project. In fact, many of those studies have gone so far as to say that reflection is the most important component. Think about the skills required to reflect. You must be able to make observations, compare and contrast your experience, and relate your experience to past experiences. Reflection allows the students to internalize what they did with what was learned.

Since the learning is internalized, it becomes important, practical, and defined. Second, students participating in service learning are making real contributions to their school and community. Not only are the students developing self-worth, but their community is developing a different perspective of our young people. Once the community has had the opportunity to interact with students, they can no longer marginalize those young people. They become legitimate members of society, not tax burdens. You will find that the community will become more supportive of you as a teacher and of your school.

How to Start a Service Learning Project

So if you are reading this section, I guess I have convinced you that service learning is a fabulous and effective teaching strategy. Good, because it is, and getting started will be less painful than you think. It is actually as easy as creating an invitation to a party. You have to think about who, what, where, when, and how. Who do you want to be involved? What issue do you want your students working on? Where and when will this project fit into your lesson plans and into the community? How will this fit into your curriculum and how will the project be evaluated?

Please remember two additional tidbits. First, involve students at every stage of the project, including planning and evaluation. Second, make sure that the students are tackling a legitimate community need. "Token" projects are doomed to fail. Kids know when you are "faking," so don't! As you might imagine, the first project is the most difficult. Once you get through one, I dare you *not* to find additional projects!

What Does Service Learning Look Like?

I must be totally honest with you. Service learning is not for the faint of heart. It takes planning and the ability to adapt and adjust at a moment's notice. It requires a teacher who is willing and able to relinquish some classroom control to the students. One of my colleagues once introduced me for a keynote address. He said, "Deb Perryman's teaching style is like an exercise in controlled chaos. There is so much movement and activity. As the occasional 'passerby,' I wonder just what she is up to. But then you see her students' final project or attend a community program and you're blown away."

Truth be known, it is the kids who blow me away. I believe that I work with the most misunderstood critter in North America, *Teenager americanis.* You are laughing because you know I am right. I have found that the best way to deal with *Teenager americanis* is to give them purpose and then get out of their way. Let me provide you with some examples.

Several years ago, two young ladies approached me with an article from the local paper. The article detailed the results of the first round of state tests as required by NCLB. Our district had eight schools on the early warning list. Six of the eight were Elgin High School Feeder Schools. These two bright-eyed juniors asked me what we were going to do to fix the problem. I scratched my head and said I had no idea, and that if I did, I would be secretary of education, a joke they did not get at all. They were serious, and I had told them all year that if they came to me with a project, I would support them.

They decided to focus on reading scores. Following the classroom procedure I had set from the beginning of the year, Rosi and Melissa taped a poster to the wall. It simply read: "Reading Score Research Team." I expected two or three students to sign up to conduct the research. To my amazement, more than 20 kids volunteered! Rosi and Melissa divided the students into research teams and gave them categories of research (libraries, Internet, reading specialist, elementary teachers, and so on).

After two weeks, the research team reported to my classes. They told us that the number one factor determining how well someone will read is whether or not the adults in their lives read aloud to the child. Rosi and Melissa looked me in the eye and firmly explained that they were going to create a reading program. They had a purpose—now came the getting out of the way!

So they planned and found community partners and classroom teachers to help them implement their reading-mentoring program. Their initial goal was to train 25 Elgin High School students to read aloud. Once their volunteers were trained, they wanted them to read at least one time in the community. They also wanted to organize a "Read Across America Night." I told them their goals were measurable and achievable.

Now came my role: I had to tie their project into my curriculum. I told them that if their trainees read children's literature with a scientific theme and developed an activity to accompany the book, I would give them credit in my environmental science class.

Rosi and Melissa then hit me with the big one: "Mrs. Perryman, we need some money to make all of this happen." I have to admit that I did cringe a bit. I was tired of selling everything that was not nailed down, but I asked what they had in mind. Rosi said that they wanted to write a grant. I thought it was a great idea and asked if they had a lead on a grant for which they wanted to apply.

Without one second of hesitation, they handed me the application for the Beyond Petroleum (BP) Leader Award Grant, funded by the U.S. subsidiary of British Petroleum, Inc. Then Melissa handed me another paper on which the pair had roughed out a budget for $27,500 for their reading program. I nearly died and I am sure my face said it all, but we decided to go for it and asked some of our community partners to help with the writing.

Rosi and Melissa had now identified three additional students to help with the grant process. They worked tirelessly, and I have to say that when it was done, I was so proud. I didn't think we had a chance of getting it, but the grant proposal was well written, measurable, and darn near a work of art. As I put it in the mail, I did a little dance by the mailbox and spun three times for luck. Four weeks later, I got a call from BP (Beyond Petroleum Inc.) telling me that we were finalists for the award. I was informed that our "team" needed to come to Chicago for an interview. We got all dressed up and headed to Chicago, ready to defend our grant.

We were ready and could answer every question BP fired at us. "How will you evaluate this? Why do you need that amount of money for this portion of the grant? How will you recognize our partnership?" We walked out of that interview with the promise of $30,000. Now I ask you, when does a classroom teacher get that amount of money, let alone more than was asked for? Never! But you have to remember, I wasn't the one who had asked. It was a team of students with a purpose.

Thanks to that seed money and the initiative of Rosi and Melissa, our reading-mentoring program is still going strong. Elgin High School will host three family reading nights this year alone. The first year, Rosi and Melissa exceeded their goal of 25 EHS students and had trained 60 to become reading mentors. Those 60 students read to more than 800 young people that first year. This school year (2005–2006), we anticipate training 300 students and hope to read to more than 2,000 local young people.

In case that example is not enough to convince you, allow me to describe the activities on our Outdoor Classroom and Nature trail. Elgin High School has a 40-acre natural area that my classes developed into a trail and classroom. Each year my students provide field trip experiences for thousands of younger learners (prekindergarten through eighth grade). Here is how it works.

Pretend that a fourth-grade teacher calls me to schedule a field trip. We agree on a day, and I select a student to serve as the "Glitch Guy/Glitch Gal." Their first official job is to call the fourth-grade teacher and ask which two state learning standards are to be met during the field experience. The Glitch Guy/Gal then relays that information to the students who have signed up to teach on that day. The high school students sign up in three groups: On-Site Activity (ecological game), Stewardship (habitat restoration), and Free Exploration. The three groups then design activities and create lesson plans to meet the standards.

On the day of the trip, the buses would pull up to our nature trail and the fourth-grade kids would file out. The Glitch Guy/Gal would welcome the elementary students, provide an overview of the day's activities, and explain the rules. Then the high school students would divide the fourth graders into three equal groups. Most of our elementary schools have three or four duplicate grades, so we could have as many as 120 elementary students on any one visit. The elementary kids are then rotated through each of the three stations, spending 30 to 40 minutes at each one. It is the responsibility of the Glitch Guy or Glitch Gal to make sure that everything runs smoothly. They handle everything from late buses to unruly participants.

I remain in the classroom teaching, but there is still plenty of adult supervision on the trip. The elementary kids are accompanied by their teachers and chaperones. The high school students are trained to talk to the elementary teachers if they feel they are in over their heads. We have yet to encounter anything that the high school kids couldn't handle. The elementary teachers really enjoy the experience and often comment on how much their students learned. Most of the elementary and middle schools we work with are Elgin High feeder schools. You can imagine the excitement of the high school student who gets to teach alongside his or her favorite elementary teacher.

In Closing

I strive to connect all classroom learning back to the community. Whether teaching elementary students the intricacies of the natural history of Illinois or reading aloud to a preschool class, my students have purpose. They are making a real-life extension into the community and learning firsthand what it takes to act as a citizen.

This is the America I want, a nation that allows kids to embrace their heritage and improve their future. The kind of America that truly teaches its young people that socioeconomic background, ethnicity, religion, and primary language do not exclude you from making a difference. That it is the right and responsibility of everyone to make our communities better. We can no longer wait until we are 40, 50, 60, or 70 to do good acts. We must begin to equip our children at younger and younger ages to do great things. The only way we improve their lives is to give them purpose.

Won't you join me in moving the young people of the United States of America to action? Learn more about service learning and how you can implement this very effective teaching strategy this school year.

Resources at Your Disposal

- Corporation for National Service/Learn and Serve America: www.nylc.org
- Illinois Campus Compact: www.illinoiscampuscompact.org
- National Service Learning Clearinghouse: www.servicelearning.org

CHAPTER 14

Environmental Studies Enhance Middle School Education

Nancy Elliott

Chillicothe, Missouri

I believe that one of the most exciting and rewarding things I have done in my teaching career is to incorporate environmental studies into our curriculum. Most of the required state and national standards can be met through environmental studies such as water quality and population studies. These studies offer ample opportunities to get the students out of the classroom and into the field to investigate what is happening in their world.

The most rewarding aspect of this manner of teaching is that it motivates and excites a wide variety of students. It is especially rewarding to see students who are not "book" students get involved in a project because they are actually doing something that someone cares about and may make a difference to people in the community or to local species of plants and animals.

Due to popular student demand, two of the environmental projects that have been long term at Chillicothe Middle School are Stream Team and the Quail Project. Stream Team is a national program sponsored by state conservation departments and the Missouri Department of Natural Resources. Students study the chemistry of water quality, biological aspects of watersheds, and the impact of human activities on the environment, and use technology to monitor water quality and educate their community about its importance. Students love going out to the river and getting wet collecting samples and looking for macro-invertebrates.

Students have reported that being a member of Stream Team changed the way they felt about school. I recently met up with a former Stream Team member, who told me that he didn't think he would have stayed in school long enough to graduate if it were not for being a part of Stream Team. To say that Tom didn't like school would be an under-statement. Tom hated school. He had few friends, wasn't involved in any extracurricular activities, didn't believe in doing homework, and skipped school every chance he had. I'm not sure when this pattern started, but it had been going on for a while. Tom had been held back twice in elementary school and was older and larger than most of the other seventh-grade students.

I kept Tom after school sometimes to make up missing work and discovered that he liked to hunt. I encouraged him to go to the river with us on our next trip, and he loved it. He enjoyed being outside and involved with nature. He knew things about the river and the fish and shared what he knew with other team members. He made friends, and I don't think he ever missed another day of school when there was a Stream Team activity.

An annual culminating activity for Stream Team members who have been active throughout the year is to go camping and canoeing. Several teachers volunteer to go along, and we visit natural and historic sites in the southern part of our state. We are fortunate to live in a state in which the top portion was once covered by glaciers and the bottom portion is rocky and has the Ozark Mountains. Students see a great diversity in the geography and streams between northern and southern Missouri. Teachers enjoy the trip because they see students in a different light when they spend three days and two nights with them—and of course students get a chance to see us differently, too. We all become more than colleagues, more than students and teachers. We return from that experience friends.

The other major project, the Quail Project, allows interested students the opportunity to evaluate northern bobwhite quail habitat and populations and develop and implement habitat improvement plans. Again, we spend nights with students so we can get up and out into the field before sunrise to take "whistle counts" of the established population. The other hours are filled with building brush piles for cover, planting food plots, and studying the plight of diminishing quail populations. Students use math and science skills and then communication skills, letting the community know what they are accomplishing.

Environmental studies lend themselves effortlessly to integration of other curricula and collaboration among teachers. A math teacher works diligently with us on math skills and is excited about the real-world application of the skills she teaches in the classroom. Students use technology to collect and evaluate data and make presentations to other students and community members.

The multitude of available resources makes teaching with environmental experiences possible. We work closely with the Missouri Department of Conservation and the Department of Natural Resources. They supply material resources and are very generous with their time, sending professionals to work with our students in the classroom and in the field.

Grants are also available to help with the funding. Our projects have been funded through Captain Planet, GreenWorks, Toyota Tapestry, Toyota TIME, the U.S. Environmental Protection Agency, the Missouri Department of Natural Resources, and several other local and state agencies.

Getting students out into the environment takes extra effort, time, and money, but the rewards are well worth it. It makes teaching and learning more fun. Students learn the required objectives and much more. They learn that they are important to the future of the environment. They become stewards of the environment for life.

CHAPTER 15

An Independent Student Research Program Implemented in a Rural Michigan Community

Jeff Shull

Armada, Michigan

A t the Macomb Academy of Arts and Sciences (MA2S) in Armada, Michigan, we have created a school for advanced math and science students that we believe is a dynamic and unique environment for optimal learning. We have created a school that provides honors-level instruction in mathematics, science, technology, and creative thinking processes embedded in the arts. We have also created a year-long independent student research program in which students follow the same processes as those followed by a university researcher.

The research program, the integration of the arts with technology, mathematics, and science, and the high-challenge/low-threat environment of MA2S are unique to our school. All decisions made at the school are based on current brain-mind research and focus on continually making the school more student centered and inquiry based.

Our research curriculum is an independent student research program that closely models the research method followed by graduate students at the university level. The student research program consists of the following eight major categories:

1. Idea generation

2. Literature review

3. Experiment design

4. Data collection

5. Data analysis

6. Mathematics and science technical writing

7. Written presentation

8. Verbal defense and presentation

The staff of the Macomb Academy of Arts and Sciences dedicates a minimum of one half day on every Wednesday schoolwide to help facilitate the student research process. This allows students to interact with the staff members who are most knowledgeable in their areas of inquiry.

Students begin the research process by working both in groups and individually to explore student-initiated questions about their everyday lives. This leads to the generation of a specific idea and hypothesis that can be tested in a laboratory setting. Students reach this goal by first compiling a list of 10 potential research topics. The list is then reviewed by individual teachers and narrowed to four topics. Students are required to write one- to two-page research proposals for all four ideas.

The proposals include details of the projects, including materials, costs, hypotheses, independent and dependent variables, constants, controls, and sample sizes. These proposals are then judged by a panel of teachers and returned to the students with a mark of accepted, rejected, or accepted with revision. Students are required to select one of their accepted proposals and present it professionally in front of a panel of experts for final review.

Understanding that the literature review of a topic should be done in advance of idea generation (we have manipulated the order of a normal research process to facilitate a high school student's time constraints, limited resources, and abilities), students are asked to create a list of 10 references about their project from sources including the Internet, magazines, books, and at least five professional journals. Students are required to follow a standard review process of all sources. In order to complete this task, students need to visit a university library.

Students are then responsible for ordering, purchasing, and setting up all experiments. It is inevitable that students encounter stumbling blocks during this portion of their research projects. Students need to develop and implement creative solutions to overcome the obstacles that they experience during the experimentation process.

A 10-week time period is allotted for students to collect data. Students are encouraged to collect as much data as possible within this time frame. Teachers closely monitor data collection to help minimize sources of error. Students are required to keep a scientific journal of their findings and submit their results on a weekly basis.

All students at the Macomb Academy of Arts and Sciences take a course during their ninth-grade year titled Design of Experiments (D.O.E.). This course is a statistics course that focuses on the analysis of student-generated data. Students apply this prior knowledge to interpret their data. They look for trends and support any conclusions made from their data using basic statistical analysis techniques. Individual groups meet with panels of teachers to refine and focus their analysis based on the students' abilities.

Next, students are introduced to technical writing, as well as peer review and critique. Each section of the students' final written papers is reviewed and critiqued by all students in their grade level as well as a primary teacher. This process repeats itself until a professional written document can be produced.

The independent student research project culminates in a final professional presentation given in front of the entire student body, teachers, parents, and invited community members. The students are required to answer questions and defend their work at the end of their presentation. Exemplary projects are submitted for competition at the national level.

When we first introduce this project every year in the fall, ninth-grade students' jaws drop in horror and awe, but by the time Thanksgiving rolls around, they are feeling relatively comfortable with the process, and after their final presentations and defenses of their research, they are immensely proud of what they have accomplished. Some of our seniors, on the other hand, have gotten so sophisticated with the projects and methods that the stress, horror, and awe are placed on the teachers to keep up with the students. In the end, everyone grows and benefits from the research program.

Helpful Tip

- Don't underestimate what can be accomplished in a small amount of time. Expect a lot from your students, your colleagues, and yourself and you will be amazed at the results.

CHAPTER 16

An Inquiry-Based, Student-Centered Approach

Jeff Shull

Armada, Michigan

I t is my goal for my students to leave my classroom with the skills and thought processes that will allow them to explore their everyday world. I want them to be able to participate in what I call "real science" versus simply following a set of mindless and meaningless directions in a prepackaged lab. More specifically, it is my hope that students in my classes will learn how to ask the next logical question about their daily experiences and then be able to develop and execute a plan of attack that will answer their question and lead to another. I want them to learn how to think like scientists.

They also need to learn how to present their findings both verbally and in written form at both an informal and at a professional level. In order to accomplish these goals, I strive daily to create a dynamic environment of high challenge and low threat both in and outside of my classroom that lends itself to optimal learning. In a perfect world, I become a facilitator, knowledgeable resource, and spectator versus a lecturer and a presenter of random facts. To an outsider, my classroom may sometimes look like organized chaos where students are participating in inquiry, differentiation, and integration, while exploring scientific phenomena for themselves and taking responsibility for their own learning.

In my classroom, I use methods similar to those used by the majority of teachers in the United States, such as lectures, labs, written reports, student presentations, projects, and assessments. For each topic that my classes learn, we use each of the aforementioned methods, but there is always a twist that immerses my students in their own learning and makes the classroom student centered. For example, the students themselves might give the lectures.

The best way to learn a topic is to teach it. Labs are usually created from scratch by the students without a set of prepackaged directions. Only a predetermined goal is given. This leads to many different explorations taking place simultaneously in the lab. Or, on the rare occasion when we do conduct classic labs with a predetermined procedure, groups of students are working on different labs that they are later required to present and teach to the rest of the class.

Writing and presentation skills are emphasized continually. If students cannot explain or express their newfound knowledge to another human being, the knowledge becomes lost. Assessments can take many forms. Sometimes it is as easy as a verbal conversation with the student. The form my students like best is to be given the opportunity to express what they have learned in any form they choose. They usually choose to make videos or PowerPoint presentations. The method of teaching that I enjoy the most is the use of open-ended, student-driven projects. The best way to demonstrate my use of these projects is by explaining some of them. The following projects are all projects that my classes have completed in this or past years during the first semester of honors physics. Projects vary from year to year based on what the students create and their interests, but I always have back-ups such as the following when we get stuck in a rut of low creativity and we need a boost in the right direction.

What Is Gravity?

Students used a tape timer to measure the acceleration of gravity and to prove that it is close to a constant value on Earth. A tape timer is a device that creates data points on a piece of paper at regular time intervals. A group of students discovered the idea of a tape timer by working with a computer program that worked on a similar principle. This led to the "What Is Gravity?" project. By attaching a mass to a piece of carbon copy tape and dropping it through a timer, the students were able to calculate the acceleration due to gravity. They discovered that if you drop a pin or a hammer, they will both fall with an acceleration of 9.8 m/s^2! I was very nervous that this exploration was going to contradict the base knowledge that we were learning in class because of the extreme amount of possible error in the experiment, but it didn't when we averaged the class's data.

Finding the Mass of a Car

This project was developed because students wanted a practical use of tape timer data. One of my students discovered a lab similar to this on the Internet, so we tried it. The idea of a tape timer was brought outside in this exploration. Students pushed a car with a constant force down a local street while dropping beanbags out of the passenger-side door at regular time intervals. The force was kept constant using simple bathroom scales! When the pushing was done, students were left with data similar to the gravity experiment. Instead of dots on a piece of tape, they had beanbags on the side of the road. From this data, we calculated the car's acceleration and then its mass using the equation force = mass × acceleration. The car's actual mass was found in the owner's manual, and we discovered that physics worked again! This led us directly into the next topic, forces and Newton's Laws.

Letterman Physics and the Speed Bus Jump

One of my students was a David Letterman fan. David Letterman, the CBS late-night talk show host, has "Physics Nights" on TV approximately twice a year. During this occasion, Letterman was throwing items out of his seventh-story window. Using free-fall equations, it was our task to calculate the true height of the seventh story. After extensive rewinding, fast-forwarding, timing, measuring, and calculating, the students discovered the window to be 68 feet from the ground.

We concluded that our answer was pretty close to the actual height, assuming a floor to be approximately 10 feet tall. This project led to a similar exploration in which we tried to calculate if the bus in the movie *Speed* could really make the miraculous jump that it made in the film. The class led themselves instinctively into the idea of projectile motion. I have also had classes analyze the forces and momentum of high school football collisions and the velocities of bricks being thrown from the roof in the movie *Home Alone*.

The Races

This project has become an annual project that all my classes perform at the beginning of the year to get their creativity flowing. In this exploration, students are asked to design a gravity-propelled "car" that will compete in seven categories: displacement, velocity, braking, accuracy, aesthetics, presentation, and report. The catch is that no premanufactured model car parts can be used in construction. Tires are made of everything from CDs to bowling balls. Brakes have included ideas that range from reverse screws to spools of thread. Extensive testing is completed, the cars are put into action, and an overall winner is determined. One year the races were even videotaped for our local cable station. This project introduces my students to all the basics of one-dimensional motion.

Independent Student Research

The project that I am most proud of and that I believe represents my teaching methods the best is a program that has been implemented throughout our school. It is a yearlong independent student research program that takes students from idea creation through publication of a scientific inquiry. The student research program consists of the following eight major categories: (1) idea generation, (2) literature review, (3) experiment design, (4) data collection, (5) data analysis,

(6) mathematics and science technical writing, (7) written presentation, and (8) verbal defense and presentation.

The independent student research program allows students to have a personal stake in their learning, which leads to the satisfaction that comes from successfully completing a task that is of high quality and that was originally thought to be above their capabilities. Students learn to see mathematics, science, and technology as rewarding fields instead of classes of rote memory and drudgery. This fosters an excitement and confidence in students to enter into mathematics, science, and technology fields in college.

The research projects are entirely student driven. Students need to be problem solvers. Teachers are used only as resources, mentors, and facilitators. During the independent research process, students encounter many additional pieces of knowledge that are not in the traditional curriculum. They are required to look ahead in the curriculum if they encounter knowledge that they have not yet learned in class. Students are asked to find creative solutions to stumbling blocks that they encounter in the research process. The research projects also allow students to use a wide range of technology and computer software.

The research process is a truly integrated process. It requires students to use mathematics, science, technology, English, art, and history in conjunction with one another. Students create projects based on real-life problems. Very few, if any, real-life problems focus on only one academic discipline. Students are challenged to inventory all their past experiences and knowledge in order to complete their independent research projects.

The research process also challenges me as a teacher more than any of the other projects. Ironically, it takes a lot of skill for a teacher to become hands-off and allow his or her students to control their own learning. The independent student research project best exemplifies all my skills as a teacher.

My greatest challenge as a teacher who attempts to make his class as student centered as possible on a daily basis is that of time management and the direction the class chooses to take as far as content is concerned. It is my responsibility as a professional educator to ensure that all the state standards are reached and treated with equal value. However, different classes, based on the questions that are posed by the students, arrive at the same final destination by following different paths. The extra effort that this style of teaching requires is well worth it. I have found that it works for all students, including those from different ability levels and personal backgrounds.

For example, it worked just as well in a suburban, general science class as it is currently working in my rural, advanced chemistry and physics classes. I also found this method of teaching successful in the past for teaching both high- and low-level math courses. I am so convinced that giving students ownership of their own learning is the most productive form of teaching that I use the same techniques when coaching basketball and sponsoring student government. Up front, I tell my players that the gym is my classroom and that what they learn and accomplish depends on them. The same is true for student government. Kids want to learn! And when they are given the reins for their own learning, as scary as it may be for the teacher, the possibilities are boundless!

Helpful Tips

- It is my belief that a teacher needs to create an environment of high challenge and low threat. The low-threat atmosphere is created through a network of respectful and caring relationships for each and every student in my classroom. It is my daily quest to create a dynamic and unique environment for my students—both in and outside the classroom—that lends itself to optimal learning. In order to accomplish this goal, I stress six expectations for both my students and myself. Students and I will strive to (1) understand real-life applications of science and math concepts; (2) respect themselves, each other, and diverse ideas; (3) apply critical and creative thinking to problem solving; (4) take responsibility for themselves and their own learning; (5) become independent thinkers and learners; and, my personal favorite, (6) be willing to take risks, make mistakes, and learn from these experiences.
- When everything clicks perfectly, the students take over and the learning is driven by the class and no longer by me. I become a facilitator and a knowledgeable resource versus a lecturer and presenter of random facts.

CHAPTER *17*

One Very Special Evening of Science

Frieda Taylor Aiken

Jackson, Georgia

C hildren are naturally curious, and Jackson Elementary School in Jackson, Georgia, takes advantage of that curiosity on one very special evening held every other year. Students return to the school with their families for a night of magical enchantment where everyone moves through the hallways exploring and experimenting. This special night is called Family Science Night, and it has become so popular that students from other schools in the county have asked permission to attend. Everyone is welcome!

Several years ago, a friend encouraged me to plan and coordinate the school's first Family Science Night. I knew that it was a job that was too big for any one person, so I took advantage of community resources that were available to our school. The most important resource, second only to the Jackson Elementary School faculty and staff, was the Georgia Youth Science and Technology Center (GYSTC). The center was able to offer assistance by providing hands-on activities for the teachers to check out from the center and use for the Family Science Night.

The activities were explained in detail and completely stocked with the materials needed to perform the activity. I planned on 40 to 50 stations set up around the school. The teachers were able to set up their activity stations just outside their classroom doors, and our principal's station always had one of the longest lines. Businesses, companies, nature centers, clubs, and government agencies were assigned tables depending on their display or activity. Contests were held and prizes were awarded for the most elaborate, most colorful, or most unique station decoration. Faculty and staff used Christmas tree lights, music, live animals, funny outfits, and catchy phrases to attract visitors. Our first Family Science Night was a huge success, and we have continued the tradition every other year.

A few of the favorite stations are as follows:

Animal Tracks. Students used rubber animal tracks to make an animal track booklet.

Paper Door. Students folded an 8-1/2' × 11' piece of paper so that they could walk through the rectangle of paper after it was cut.

Drops of Water on a Penny. Students used a pipette to determine how many drops of water would stay on the surface of a penny. Prizes were awarded for the student who managed to get the most drops to stay on the penny's surface.

Build a Barge. Students used aluminum foil to build a barge that would hold pennies. They held a contest to see which barge could hold the most pennies. Prizes were awarded for the barges that held the most pennies.

Cat's Meow. Students dropped food coloring into a plate of milk at 12:00, 3:00, 6:00, and 9:00 o'clock. Then the students touched a toothpick that had been dipped in dishwashing detergent into the center of the milk. The detergent began to break up the fat in the milk, and the food coloring began to swirl.

Static Electricity With Balloons. Students rubbed balloons onto their hair, and they touched the balloon to rice cereal.

Silly Putty. Students used white school glue and a borax-and-water solution to make "silly putty."

Put a Child Into a Bubble. Students stood inside a tractor tire that had been filled with a bubble solution. A hula hoop was dipped into the bubble solution, and the hula hoop was lifted up and over the student.

Paper Clip Pickup. Students made an electromagnet and used it to see how many paper clips they could pick up.

Rock Identification. Students used a dichotomous key to identify rocks.

Fossils. Students used fossil books to identify fossils.

Tree Rings. Students used tree rings to determine the age and changes in the life of a tree.

Make Music With Bottles of Water. Students used glass soda bottles to make music. They filled the bottles to different levels with water and matched the sounds that each bottle made to a chart. They played a simple song using the bottles.

Make Your Own Kazoo. Students made their own kazoos using straws.

Drop of Water Race. Students raced using drops of water on a piece of waxed paper.

Owl Pellets. Students dissected owl pellets to determine what the owl had eaten.

Other stations or demos include the following:

Elephant Toothpaste Demo. Dishwashing detergent, green food coloring, lab-grade hydrogen peroxide, sodium iodide (NaI) crystals, and a

500-mL graduated cylinder were used to produce a very foamy substance, which looks like toothpaste coming out of a huge tube.

Star Lab. GYSTC brought Star Lab to the school and provided a person to teach a lesson inside the Star Lab.

A Giant Whale You Can Walk Inside. GYSTC brought a giant "whale" made from black plastic garbage bags. It was blown up with huge fans, and the students could walk inside the "whale" to understand the size of the animal.

Van de Graaff Generator Station. The generator produces static electricity, and the students got their pictures taken with their hair standing on end.

Telescope Station. A professor from a nearby university brought a telescope for the students to look through. He also had one of the longest lines.

High School Science Teacher. A high school colleague set up a station with microscopes and live animals.

Middle School Science Team. A group of middle school students conducted multiple experiments.

4-H Club. Club members set up an activity teaching the students about bees.

Charlie Elliott Wildlife Center and Dauset Trails Nature Center. Nearby nature centers brought live animals and animal artifacts.

Indian Springs State Park. A nearby state park brought Native American artifacts.

Local Companies. One of the best lessons was taught by a milk company, and the company supplied free chocolate milk to each student who attended the session.

Helpful Tips

- First sell the idea of a Family Science Night to your administration and then to your faculty. You must have the support of those two important groups for the night to be a success.
- Make yourself and your Family Science Night Team available, and let your faculty know that you are willing to help. Teachers have enough to do already, and they do not need to be responsible for gathering supplies or equipment.
- You and your team of Family Science Night experts will need to help with everything from setup to takedown. The team will also need to plan where all the stations will be placed so that a map for the night can be created.
- Make Family Science Night a night of fun that is exciting and stress-free for all.

Index